Table of Contents

Foreword

I've had the pleasure of knowing Nathaniel — or Nat, as he's commonly known around the industry —for the past decade, but truth be told, it feels like we've known each other a lot longer. Working in different businesses but with nearly identical target audiences, it was inevitable that we'd run into each other over the years. Almost immediately it was clear the similarities that connected us, whether it was both of us being family men, both working to assist the construction industry, or that we both have a similar philosophy in our approach to that work. Above all, though, what really brought us together was the fact that Nat cares, and that's something that too often gets left by the wayside in business.

Nat cares deeply for his wife and children, and he really does believe in "family first" above everything else. He's grounded and has strong values — important characteristics in what we do. It makes him the type of guy that you can trust, and he brings that same level of dedication into his work. It's why his guidance is sought after throughout the entire industry.

Working in the construction software business, I deal with a lot prevailing wage and fringe tracking — Nat's area of expertise. It's caused us to cross paths a lot over the years. Beyond Nat being the guy I and just about every other association get in touch with if I have a question on an obscure prevailing wage rule, I consider myself lucky to call him a friend — primarily because he cares about the people he works with, whether a colleague or client. We share a common belief that, even more than making a sale, we want to help contractors run the best businesses that they can. We want to educate them on the business practices, software, and tools that can help them elevate their businesses to the next level — and that's exactly what Nat does within this book.

Nat also cares about being the best in his field. Because of this, he's respected across the industry and is a go-to subject-matter expert in the field of prevailing wage. You can often find him out on the road, presenting at conferences to help educate contractors of every trade on fringe benefits and packages. And along with helping contractors to streamline their businesses and processes, he also makes sure their employees reap the rewards as well by walking them through individual tax benefits they can use and ways they can start saving for retirement.

This book represents an extension of Nat's research and expertise. It's an invaluable tool for contractors and other industry professionals who want a detailed look at the history and impact of the Davis-Bacon Act — and nobody knows this topic better than Nat.

In my experience, I've found that too frequently contractors end up avoiding government work altogether because of how complicated reporting requirements can be. That's where Nat, and particularly this book, can help. With his detailed exploration of all aspects of the Davis-Bacon Act, he's able to break down the text of the Act — and explain all of its subsequent requirements and nuances — into an easily digestible, yet incredibly thorough, thesis on the Davis-Bacon Act and all of the complexities that come along with it. All of this is because Nat cares about making government work accessible to contractors.

This book was much needed in the industry, and I can't think of a single person more qualified to write it than Nat. His contributions and efforts to educate his audience, as well as the care with which he presents them, are critical to the industry.

Steve Antill
Chief Revenue Officer
Foundation Software

Introduction

This book reviews the history of the Davis-Bacon Act (DBA) and explains the requirements for compliance with state and federal prevailing-wage regulations and reporting.

Each chapter stands on its own. Readers can select specific chapters to meet their needs and read them in any order. Some will find the book informative and read it "cover-to-cover." Others may choose to read select chapters based on their immediate need.

Above all, this book is a concise record of the most vital information related to the DBA and includes essential information for any construction contractor doing federal, state, or local government funded work subject to prevailing wage legislation.

Robert L. Bacon

Robert Low Bacon was born July 23, 1884, in the aristocratic Dorchester Center neighborhood of Boston. As the firstborn of Martha and Robert Bacon Sr., their son was a student at the local public schools before gaining admission to Harvard University. He graduated with a bachelor's degree in 1907. Three years later he received a Juris Doctorate from Harvard Law School.

Bacon's father was a successful investment banker in partnership with J.P. Morgan, and later briefly served as acting United States Secretary of State and as Ambassador to France during the President Theodore Roosevelt administration.

Bacon was a gregarious and outgoing man with the nickname "Prince Charming." He was an active member of many fraternal organizations including the American Legion, Freemasons, Knights Templar, Shriners International, The Benevolent and Protective Order of Elks, and the Loyal Order of Moose. Active in the military, Bacon served at the Texas border with the New York National Guard in 1916. A few years later, during the First World War, he served with the United States Army as part of the American Expeditionary Force. During his service, Bacon reached the rank of major and received the Distinguished Service Medal.

Bacon's political career began as a representative to several New York State conventions. He later served as a delegate to the 1920 Republican National Convention held in Chicago. He was first elected to Congress as a Republican from NY and served eight terms beginning on March 4, 1923 until his death on September 12, 1938 from a heart attack. Bacon was laid to rest at Arlington National Cemetery.

James J. Davis

James John Davis was born in Wales in 1873 to Esther and David Davies. He immigrated to the United States with his parents at the age of eight. His parents changed their name to Davis on their arrival, but James would later sign his last name "Davies" even though his legal name was Davis.

Davis began his career at the age of eleven withstanding laborious twelve-hour workdays in the heat and fumes to create wrought iron. He was later known as "Pudler Jim" because of these early formative experiences. He joined the *Amalgamated Association of Iron, Steel, and Tin Workers of America* where he held various positions and later authored a book called *The Iron Puddler: My Life in the Rolling Mills and What Came of It.*

Active in the *Loyal Order of Moose*, Davis, like Robert Bacon, was a gregarious and friendly person. He served as Secretary of Labor from 1921 to 1930 under Presidents Warren G. Harding, Calvin Coolidge, and Herbert Hoover. He is one of only three Cabinet officers in U.S. history to hold the same post under three consecutive Presidents. He resigned as Secretary of Labor to be seated as the Republican Senator from Pennsylvania, where he served three terms until 1944.

Passage of the Davis-Bacon Act

The act was designed to counter various practices which occurred in the wake of the rapid expansion of federal construction projects. For example, contractors in cheap labor areas were able to underbid contractors where a higher wage rate prevailed and import their own work force, resulting in the unemployment of local labor, inability of local contractors to compete against distant ones for jobs in their own region, and the depression of local wage standards.[1]

---

[1] James H. Watz, Labor Law, 6 B.C.L. Rev. 242 (1965), http://lawdigitalcommons.bc.edu/bclr/vol6/iss2/8

During hearings before the House Committee on Labor in February 1927, Representative Bacon introduced legislation to require locally prevailing wage standards be met in federal construction work. The issue had emerged during construction of a federal Veteran's Bureau hospital in Bacon's New York district. Local contractors, he explained, had submitted bids on the project that reflected local standards. But the contract was awarded to an Alabama firm. The contractor, Bacon noted,

> *"... brought some thousand non-union laborers from Alabama into Long Island, N.Y.; ... They were herded onto this job, they were housed in shacks, they were paid a very low wage and the work proceeded."*

Bacon believed the least the government could do when contracting was,

> *"to comply with the local standards of wages and labor prevailing in the locality where the building construction is to take place."*

His measure did not seek to inflate wages artificially but, rather, to assure that government respect the existing local standard of pay. The bill was not adopted. Over the next few years Bacon attempted to introduce variations on the prevailing wage bill 13 times, all of which were unsuccessful.[2,3] Finally, in the midst of the Great Depression, local worker complaints about imported cheap labor took on a new urgency with unprecedented rates of unemployment. The Hoover Administration requested that Congress reconsider the Act as a means of elevating wages.[4] Congress obliged seeking higher wages and employment in their districts and paid for by the federal government.[5]

Sponsored in the Senate by former Labor Secretary James Davis, the legislation passed by voice vote and was signed into law on March 3rd, 1931.[6]

[2] Bernstein, David, *The Davis-Bacon Act: Let's Bring Jim Crow to an End* (PDF), Cato Institute

[3] Schulman, Stuart, "The Case Against the Davis-Bacon Act", *Government-Union Review* (Winter 1983)

[4] Glassman, Sarah; Head, Michael; Tuerck, David G.; Bachman, Paul (2008), *The Federal Davis-Bacon Act: The Prevailing Mismeasure of Wages* (PDF), Beacon Hill Institute

[5] Bernstein, David E. (2001), "Prevailing-Wage Laws", *Only One Place of Redress: African Americans, Labor Regulations and the Court from Reconstruction to the New Deal*, Duke University Press, ISBN 978-0822325833

[6] Whittaker, William G. (13 November 2007), *Davis-Bacon: The Act and The Literature, Report 94-908*(PDF), Congressional Research Service

The Davis-Bacon Act

The Davis-Bacon Act (DBA) requires the minimum wage payment of "prevailing" rates as determined by the Department of Labor (DOL) Wage and Hour Division (WHD) to all laborers and mechanics on federal government construction (including alteration and/or repair) on projects in all fifty states and the District of Columbia for contracts in excess of $2,000. Construction includes painting and decorating public works or buildings under a federal, or *federally assisted*, contract **except** for where the assistance is solely in the nature of a loan guarantee or insurance.

The Department of Labor (DOL) has published instructions and rules in the Code of Federal Regulations (CFR) specifically in Title 29 CFR. The following key parts provide guidance on and establish "rules of the road" for:

Part 1: DBA wage determinations, including instructions on how to use the determinations

Part 3: Copeland Act requirements for weekly of submission Certified Payroll Reports (CPR)

Part 5: DBA labor standards, wage rates and contractor responsibilities

Part 6: Administrative and enforcement procedures, including the withholding of payment

Part 7: Boundaries for practice before the **Administrative Review Board** (previously known as the Wage Appeals Board)

Davis-Bacon Amendments of 1935

The initial Davis-Bacon Act (DBA) signed into law in 1931, but was not clear on how contracts were supposed to state "the minimum wages to be paid various classes of laborers and mechanics."

In 1935, the first amendment to the DBA occurred, for the first time providing contractors with a guaranteed predetermination of the wage rate. In other words, the contractor would know the mandated hourly pay rates in advance of bid submission by the contractor.

The 1935 amendment also reduced the project's financial threshold to $2,000, from $5,000, ensuring that virtually all federal projects were subject to DBA requirements.

Davis-Bacon Related Acts

The Davis-Bacon Related Acts (DBRA) applied extended Davis-Bacon requirements to numerous "related Acts" that provide federal assistance. In contrast with direct federal contracts, DBRA are **indirect** contracts for construction services provided to a private entity but funded with government dollars.

Examples of public funding may include:
- Grants
- Loan Guarantees
- Loans
- Insurance

Contractors will see instances of DBRA in the form of Housing & Urban Development (HUD) financed construction of low-income housing projects or Federal Highway Administration (FHA) provided grants to states for construction of highways and bridges.

Wage Determinations

The Davis-Bacon Act (DBA) wage determinations are comprised of three basic elements:[7]

- The prevailing wage reflects rates paid on **"projects of a similar character,"** i.e. Building, Residential, Highway & Heavy.

- "Locality" for the Wage Determination (WD) is established by the "city, town, village, or other civil subdivision of the state in which the work is... performed." **County is typically used.**

- The **"prevailing wage"** includes both wages and bona fide fringe benefits.

The accuracy of wage determinations developed from survey data is *"dependent upon interested party participation."*[8]

It is interesting to note, that

---

[7] 29 CFR 1.3

[8] Presentation of Davis Bacon Wage Survey Process –
https://www.dol.gov/whd/programs/dbra/wd-10.htm

"Prevailing wage laws <u>establish a wage floor</u>, they raise construction costs. The reason is twofold: First, the wage that "prevails" in a particular place at any snapshot in time might be greater than the wage that contractors would have to pay if, for example, they could hire cheaper labor from outside the area. Indeed, as we observe in our study, it is the very possibility that employers could hire cheaper labor that led to the passage of the DBA in the first place. Second, because the law is intended to <u>reduce wage competition</u>, the government authorities responsible for calculating the prevailing wage are under pressure to use methods for calculating the wage that are biased upward." [9]

The following are some of the worker classifications of laborers or mechanics covered under the Davis-Bacon Act:

- Carpenters
- Electricians
- Plumbers

---

[9] BHI/ The Prevailing Mismeasure of Wages - http://www.beaconhill.org/BHIStudies/PrevWage08/DavisBaconPrevWage080207Final.pdf

- Ironworkers
- Flaggers
- Craftsmen
- Welders
- Concrete Finishers
- Longshoremen
- Power Equipment Operators
- Helpers

Conversely, the following is a list of some of the worker classifications generally NOT covered under by DBA:

- Architects
- Engineers
- Timekeepers
- Supervisors
- Foremen
- Workers performing exploratory drilling services, such as subsurface utility engineering or utility location services, for the purpose of obtaining data to be used in engineering studies and the planning of a project. (The work performed is related to an activity and not a project; therefore the DBRA does not apply.)
- Employees of railroads, public utilities, and public agency employees performing work

- Survey crew members using the equipment for measuring heights, distances, and bearings.
- Owner-Operators of trucks who drive their own trucks (The certified payroll would indicate that the work was performed by named "owner-operator" but would not need to show hours worked or the rate of pay).

The DBA wage decision is simply a listing of the various work classifications and the minimum wage rate that must be paid to anyone performing work in those classifications. While this sounds simple, in practice, a certain employee / worker may serve in several different capacities within a single workday. For instance, in Los Angeles County, the installation of conduit, boxes, cables, and devices is performed at the Inside Wireman rate, but the final connection and programming is performed at the Communication and System Installer rate, which is a 47% higher per hour wage rate.

Contractors are encouraged to complete the Department of Labor (DOL) Wage and Hour Division (WHD) form WD-10, which can be found here:
https://whd.dol-esa.gov/wd10/wd10.do

Certified Payroll Reports

Contractors are required to submit a weekly Certified Payroll Reports (CPR) beginning with the first week the contractor works on the project. Every week thereafter, a weekly report is required even if no work occurs. "It's always a good idea to number the payroll reports beginning with #1 and to clearly mark your last payroll for the project "Final."[10] It is also a best practice to submit a note to the contracting officer that no work was done on a job in a given week or to submit a "no work" certified payroll report.

Payrolls and basic time records must be maintained and preserved as required by 29 CFR 5.5(a)(3) and 48 CFR 52.222-8. 29 CFR 3.3, 29 CFR 3.4, and 29 CFR 5.5(a)(3) contain the reporting requirements relative to submission of the weekly Statement of Compliance and payrolls to the contracting agency. Contractors and subcontractors on DBRA covered construction projects must submit each week a "Statement of Compliance," which certifies the contractor's compliance with the DBRA requirements.

---

[10] *Contractor's Guide to Davis-Bacon 2-2*

This "Statement of Compliance" is usually referred to as the Certified Payroll Report (CPR). The contractor must submit a weekly copy of all payrolls to the contracting agency. The payroll information may be submitted to DOL in various ways, including paper and electronically, but must provide a complete and accurate accounting of all required information. One option is form WH-347, a WHD form available to contractors on http://www.wdol.gov.

The prime contractor is responsible for submission of the certified payrolls to the contracting agency. Each payroll submitted must be accompanied by a Statement of Compliance which is found on the reverse side of the WH-347. The contractor or subcontractor must make the payroll records available for inspection, copying, or transcription by authorized representatives of the contracting agency or the DOL and must permit these representatives to interview workers during working hours on the job. If the contractor or subcontractor fails to submit the required records or to make them available, the federal agency may, after written notice to the contractor, take such action as is necessary to cause suspension of any further payment, advance or guarantee of funds. Failure to submit the required records upon request or to make such records available may be grounds for debarment action.

CPRs must be retained for a minimum of three (3) years after the project is completed.

Calculating Labor Rates

The Davis-Bacon Act (DBA) requires the Secretary of Labor to predetermine, as a monetary wage, the prevailing wage rates for corresponding classes of laborers and mechanics employed on projects of a character similar to the contract work in the area where work is to be performed. Bona fide fringe benefits are included within the meaning of the terms "wages, scale of wages, wage rates, minimum wages, and prevailing wages," as used in the DBA. See 40 USC 3141 and 29 CFR 5.2(p).

Since the passage of the DBA, the calculation of the local labor "prevailing-wage" rate has been heatedly debated. Under the act, the Department of Labor (DOL) is tasked with developing the wage rates based on the locale, usually county, the work is to be conducted in as well as the job classification. The DOL has been blamed for its use of a complex system "unscientific methods" to estimate prevailing wage rates.

> *GAO revealed problems with accuracy, quality, bias and timeliness of the wage data. Of the surveys reviewed, one in four of the final wage rates were based on the wages of just six or fewer workers.*[11]

Specifically, the Wage & Hour Division (WHD) of the Department of Labor conducts surveys through its five regional offices. Data is compiled from contractors and "other interested parties" (i.e. unions) on form WD-10. Certified payrolls may supplement the WD-10 data. Wages are recorded per job classification within four major categories:

Building: sheltered enclosures with walk-in access for the purpose of housing persons, machinery, equipment, or supplies. This category includes all construction of such structures, the installation of equipment, as well as incidental grading and paving. Such structures need not be habitable to be building construction. Examples of building construction projects are auditoriums, city halls, apartment buildings (five stories and above), hospitals, office buildings, schools, warehouses, and shopping centers.

Residential: single family houses or apartment buildings of four stories or less.

Highway: alteration or repair of roads, streets, highways, runways, alleys, trails, paths, parking areas, and other similar projects not incidental to building or heavy construction.

---

11   https://www.govinfo.gov/content/pkg/CHRG-112hhrg65695/pdf/CHRG-112hhrg65695.pdf

<u>Highway Construction</u>: Includes construction, alteration or repair of roads, streets, highways, runways, taxiways, alleys, trails, paths, parking areas, and other similar projects not incidental to building or heavy construction.

<u>Heavy</u>: This is a catch-all category. It includes all other projects not classified as building, highway or residential (e.g., bridges over navigable waters, dams, tunnels, and dredging / irrigation projects). Of the four categories of construction, this is the only type of construction that can be broken into subcategories such as water and sewer line projects and dredging projects.

Worker Classification Conformance

Work classifications are not always inclusive of the work being done and it can be appropriate for the contractor to create an additional "trade" classification with a unique wage rate. For example, one electrical contractor won a solar installation job. Part of the installation was removing solar panels from cardboard packaging on arrival from the manufacturer. Since there was no job classification for "solar packaging removal specialist," the contractor created the role, wrote it up and submitted it for review. The approval saved the contractor tens of thousands of dollars not having to pay an electrician at the prevailing wage rate to unpack boxes of solar panels.

According to the *Contractor's Guide to Davis-Bacon...*

> *Basically, you identify the classification you need and recommend a wage rate for DOL to approve for the project. There are a few of rules about additional classifications; you'll find these rules in the DOL regulations, Part 5, and in the labor clauses of your contract. The rules are summarized for you here:*
>
> *1) The requested classification is used by construction*

contractors in the area of the project, usually defined as the County.

2) *The work that will be performed by the requested classification is not already performed by another classification that is already on the wage decision. (In other words, if there is already an Electrician classification and wage rate on the wage decision, you can't request another Electrician classification and rate.)* [12]

---

[12] *Contractor's Guide to Davis-Bacon*

Definition of "Laborer" & Wage Classifications

DBA regulations refer to "laborers and mechanics," but the definition of who is subject to the law is not always clear. At a high level, laborers includes:

- Workers whose duties are manual or physical in nature
- Includes apprentices, trainees, and helpers
- For CWHSSA, includes watchmen and guards

Does Not Include:

- Timekeepers, inspectors, architects, engineers
- Bona fide executive, administrative, and professional employees as defined under FLSA
- Working foremen are generally non-exempt. If not FLSA 541 exempt, must be paid the DB rate for the classification of work performed.

Contractors must designate the correct work classification based on the actual work performed pursuant to the wage determination "scope of work." For instance, if an employee is performing work as a carpenter, that worker may be paid no less than the prevailing wage rate of carpenter *irrespective of the carpenter's skill level*.

A worker can work in two or more classifications during a workweek and be paid at two or more Base Hourly Rate (BHR) and Fringe Benefit (FB) rates. This frequently occurs when a contractor has work in multiple jurisdictions, i.e. different locales or states, with different wage rates. The same carpenter could have different wage rates within the same day depending on the jobsites he or she is assigned to.

Example:

- A worker works 15 hours performing electrical work pursuant to the scope of work of an "inside wireman" at an BHR of $60 and FB of $20 totaling $80 / hour and 25 hours as a Comm & System Installer at a BHR of $40 BHR and $10 FB totaling $50 / hr.

- The applicable WD wage and fringe benefit for each classification is paid for the hours worked in each classification.

- The time cards must accurately reflect the hours worked in each scope of work classification
  - Inside Wireman
    - 15 hours x BHR of $60 = $900
    - 15 hours x FB of $20 = $300
  - Comm. & System Installer

- 25 hours x BHR of $40 = $1,000
- 25 hours x FB of $10 = $250
  - Total
    - 40 hours BHR of $1,900 (i.e. paycheck)
      - 40 hours FB of $550 (i.e. bona fide benefits)

Fringe Benefits

In 1964, Congress completed action on an Administration-backed bill (HR 6041) amending the Davis-Bacon Act to include fringe benefits in the determination of prevailing wages. The Committee said there had been "a tremendous change in the concept of earnings since Congress enacted the Davis-Bacon Act." Fringe benefit plans "were the rare exception in the 1930s," but were now prevalent and should be included if the Act "is to continue to accomplish its purpose."[13] Fringe benefits which are specifically authorized include:

- Medical / health insurance
- Retirement benefits
- Life insurance
- Holiday / Vacation / Sick / Personal Time Off (PTO)
- Apprenticeship training funds

The prevailing wage obligation may be satisfied by:

- Paying the Basic Hourly Rate (BHR) and Fringe Benefit (FB) in cash;
- Contributing payments to a bona fide plan; or
- Any combination of the two

---

[13] "Davis-Bacon Amendments." In CQ ALMANAC 1964, 20th ed., 576-77. Washington, DC: Congressional Quarterly, 1965. http://library.cqpress.com/cqalmanac/cqal64-1303410.

Cash wages paid in excess of the BHR may offset or satisfy the FB obligation or alternatively the contractor may "dip into the base" and have fringes that exceed the fringe allocation.

For example, a contractor may comply by paying:

BHR $30 per hour
FB $10 per hour
=======
       $40 - total PW obligation

a) $40 per hour in the paycheck
b) $35 per hour in the paycheck plus $5 in FB
c) $29 per hour in the paycheck and $11 per hour in FB

Fringe benefit requirements will sometimes be represented as a percentage on the wage determination and compliance is achieved by calculating the percentage times the dollar amount of the basic wage rate. For example, a fringe rate of 25% would be multiplied by a basic hourly wage of $50 to achieve a $12.50 per hour fringe obligation. **Fringe benefits are required on all hours worked.**

For contractors to take credit as offering a bona fide benefit without prior approval from DOL, the following must occur:

1) Communicated to an eligible employee in writing

2) Contributions must be made irrevocably
3) Contributions must be made on a regular and frequent basis (**not less than quarterly**)

The WHD Field Operations Handbook, section 15f11(f) states, ***"The contractor is under no obligation to obtain the employee's concurrence before contributing to the fringe benefit plan on his or her behalf."*** In other words, the contractor's contribution of fringes into a bona fide plan is an employer decision.

Annualization

Generally, prevailing wage fringe benefit plan contributions **may not** be used to fund a benefits plan during periods of non-government work.[14] The WHD here has created a policy, sometimes referred to as "annualization," that reflects the strategy of determining an effective annual rate for all hours worked – both public and private.

DOL developed this policy based on their view of legislative intent; Congress did not intend to have government funds utilized to pay for benefits that are received during periods of private (non-prevailing wage) work. Annualization prevents contractors from using prevailing wage fringes to fund benefits that are **continuous in nature**, employers must fund these benefits for all hours of work, both public and private.

Annualization Example

	PW Hours	Private Hours	Fringe ($10/hr)	Health Cost	Per Hour Credit
Q1	500	0	$5,000	$1,200	$3
Q2	0	500		$1,200	

---

[14] FOH 15f11, see also FOH 15f12(b)

Q3	0	500		$1,200	
Q4	0	500		$1,200	

Let's assume that in the first quarter (Q1) an employee works 500 hours on a prevailing wage job with a fringe mandate of $10 per hour resulting in a fringe obligation of $5,000. The rest of the year the employee only works on private (non-PW) work. Let's also assume that the employer cost for health insurance is $400 per month ($1,200 per month or $4,800 per year).

The fringes payable in Q1 would provide the contractor with enough funds to pay for health insurance for the entire year (with $200 left over) even though nine of the twelve months were working on private work.

In order to remedy situations where government fringes would otherwise be funding private work benefits, the DOL mandates the amortization of health insurance (and other ongoing benefits such as dental, vision, life, disability, etc.) on a per hour basis.

The most commonly used formula is:
Hourly Rate = Monthly Premium divided by 2080 [40 hrs. per week x 52 weeks]

Other versions of the formula include number of hours worked in a prior month or average hours worked in a prior year instead of 2080 as the divisor.

Pension Plan Annualization Exception

The exception came about pursuant to a change in policy by DOL in 1984. Per the DOL Wage Appeals Board decision in Dyad Construction:[15]

> *DOL policy is that employers are prohibited from using fringe benefit contributions made for work covered by the Davis-Bacon Act to fund employee benefits for periods of non-Davis-Bacon work. Under the changed policy, DOL has decided that a defined contribution pension plan which meets the following criteria does not use contributions credited for Davis-Bacon work to fund the plan during non-Davis-Bacon work, even if the contribution rates are different for covered and non-covered work.*

---

[15] Case No. 84-15

To qualify for this exception to Annualization, the defined contribution pension plan must provide:

- Immediate participation and
- Essentially immediate vesting (100% vesting after an employee works 500 or fewer hours, which means that the contributions are made irrevocably by the contractor)

This exception allows full credit (all dollars contributed) for the amount of contributions made on Davis-Bacon work.

Piece Rate/Work

"Piece rate," sometimes known as "piece work," is where an employee's earnings are based on a factor of the work produced. It is important to note that the employee must be paid at least (_not less than_) the prevailing wage rate for their worker classification for the hours worked.

For instance, if a sheetrock installer is paid per board of sheetrock installed, the installer must still earn more on an hourly basis than the hourly prevailing wage rate. Employers must calculate the hourly earnings and ensure that the "piece work" compensation exceeds the per hour wage rate including actual hours and overtime (O/T).

In order to determine the basic hourly rate for a piece rate employee, it is necessary to divide the total hours worked on the job into the total wages paid and this calculation must be done weekly.[16]

---

[16] FOH 15f10

Project Labor Agreements (PLA)

The term "project labor agreement" refers to a pre-hire collective bargaining agreement with one or more labor organizations that establishes the terms and conditions of employment for a specific construction project.

Groups including the Associated General Contractors of America (AGC), Associated Builders and Contractors (ABC), Construction Industry Roundtable (CIRT), National Federation of Independent Business (NFIB), the National Black Chamber of Commerce, and the U.S. Chamber of Commerce have actively opposed the use of PLAs, particularly for government projects.[17]

Generally, those opposed to PLAs argue PLAs are a special interest scheme that discourage fair competition from non-union contractors by requiring a project to be awarded only to contractors and subcontractors that agree to recognize unions as the representatives of their employees on that job; use the union hall to obtain workers; obey the union's restrictive apprenticeship and

---

[17] https://www.nationalbcc.org/news/latest-news/2895-coalition-letter-to-peotus-trump-on-project-labor-agreement-policy

work rules; and contribute to union pension plans and other funds in which their non-union employees will never benefit unless they join a union.[18]

Additionally, organizations opposed to PLAs cite, *"multiple studies of hundreds of taxpayer-funded school construction projects found PLA mandates increase the cost of construction between 12 percent and 18 percent compared to similar non-PLA projects."*[19]

Proponents of PLAs argue, among other benefits of organized labor, that the agreements have several advantages:

1. Uniform wages, benefits, overtime pay, hours, working conditions, and work rules for work on major construction projects.
2. Prevent labor strife by prohibiting strikes and lockouts while including binding procedures to resolve labor disputes.
3. Make large projects easier to manage by placing unions under one contract, the PLA, rather than dealing with several unions that

---

[18]   https://www.smithcurrie.com/publications/common-sense-contract-law/project-labor-agreements-in-public-and-private-contracting/

[19]   https://www.nationalbcc.org/news/latest-news/2895-coalition-letter-to-peotus-trump-on-project-labor-agreement-policy

may have different wage and benefit structures.[20]

If one is pro-union, then PLAs are a natural extension of organized labor's bona fides. However, merit-shop contractors, whose employees make up 87.2% of the construction workforce, are against PLAs.

According to ABC,

> *Ninety-eight percent of survey respondents said they were less likely to bid on a taxpayer-funded construction contract if the bid specifications required the winning firm to sign a PLA with labor unions, and 97 percent of survey respondents said a construction contract that required a PLA would be more expensive compared to a contract procured via free and open competition.[21]*

In essence, one's view of PLAs will likely be constrained by ones view of unionization.

---

[20] https://www.cga.ct.gov/2011/rpt/2011-R-0360.htm

[21] https://thetruthaboutplas.com/2019/01/30/survey-abc-members-strongly-oppose-government-mandated-project-labor-agreements/

The non-partisan Congressional Research Service issued a report on PLAs on July 1, 2010, indicating the evidence is inconclusive regarding the cost of PLAs on construction projects.[22]

---

[22] Project Labor Agreements, CRS R41310

General "Prime" Contractors

Is this us if we are serving?

The General "Prime" Contractor (GC) is responsible for the full and complete compliance of all "sub-contractors" and lower tier-contractors. The liability for all hourly employees to be paid the correct wages lies with the GC who is contractually responsible.

GC's should review the Certified Payroll Report (CPR) for each sub-contractor for each week to ensure compliance; simply receiving and retaining records is insufficient. The GC must retain all CPRs, including those of sub-contractors, for a minimum of three (3) years after the project is completed.

All prevailing wage compliance questions should be funneled up through the GC to the contract administrator.

See the chapter *"**Penalties for Non-compliance**"* for details, but both the sub-contractor and GC are liable for penalties for non-compliance.

Diversity and Inclusion Programs

Congress has established a 23% government wide goal for awards of contracts to small businesses. Subsets of the small business goal are a 5% government wide goal for awards to small disadvantaged businesses (SDBs), a 5% government wide goal for awards to women-owned small businesses (WOSB), a 3% government wide goal for awards to a historically underutilized small businesses (HUBZone), and a 3% government wide goal for awards to service-disabled veteran-owned small businesses (SDVOSB). A contract can get counted towards more than one goal: an award to an SDB in a HUBZone that is owned by a service-disabled woman veteran would be counted towards all the goals.[23]

8(a) Business Development program

The federal government's goal is to award at least 5% percent of all federal contracting dollars to small disadvantaged businesses each year.

> *Socially disadvantaged individuals are those who have been subjected to racial or ethnic prejudice or cultural bias within American society because of their identities as members of groups*

---

[23] https://www.fedgovcontracts.com/chap11.pdf

and without regard to their individual qualities.[24]

Service-Disabled Veteran-Owned Small Businesses program (SDVOB)

The federal government's goal is to award at least 3% of all federal contracting dollars to service-disabled veteran-owned small businesses each year.

Women-Owned Small Business Federal Contracting program

The federal government's goal is to award at least 5% of all federal contracting dollars to women-owned small businesses each year.

HUBZone program

The federal government's goal is to award at least 3% of all federal contracting dollars to HUBZone-certified small businesses each year.

Disadvantaged Business Enterprise (DBE) Program

Department of Transportation (DOT)

---

[24] https://www.ecfr.gov/cgi-bin/text-idx?SID=7ae1f410a0cc51b5054e09676ad67ae6&mc=true&node=se13.1.124_1103&rgn=div8

Supplemental Unemployment Benefits

Supplemental Unemployment Benefits, also known as "SUB" plans, arose out of attempts by labor unions to negotiate guaranteed worker wages.

The first SUB plans were negotiated in the automobile industry in 1955, and the bulk of the plans developed since that time have followed their general pattern. Under these plans a worker is eligible for SUB payments if laid off by the company, either in a reduction in force or in a temporary layoff. Usually these payments also depend on the concurrent receipt (at least during part of the period) of state unemployment benefits. In addition, an *employee has no vested interest in amounts the employer pays into the fund*, and if the employee leaves the company voluntarily or is discharged for misconduct, he/she is not eligible for a benefit.[25]

---

[25] Senate Report No. 1518, 1960–2 C.B. 753 at 754.

While SUB plans have existed for many years, the prevalence of these programs being offered by prevailing wage contractors has grown since the early 2000's. A number of SUB plans have received a U.S. Department of Labor, Wage and Hour Division exemption from the Davis-Bacon Act's annualization requirement as well as a handful of state-level exemptions.

"Unemployment benefits" are explicitly mentioned in the Davis-Bacon Act regulations and, when used appropriately, can be of real value to employees during actual periods of unemployment. However, employers should consider a key topic when considering a SUB plan: taxation. IRC 501(c)(9) exempts SUB plans from federal income tax. However, a 2014 Supreme Court decision, Quality Stores, affirmed that SUB benefits *must be linked to the receipt of state unemployment benefits* and the amounts paid cannot vary based upon seniority and years of service. Otherwise, amounts would be considered wages subject to FICA and FUTA.

A SUB plan must provide for supplemental unemployment benefits paid only because of an employee's involuntary separation from employment, whether temporary or permanent,

    (i)   resulting directly from a reduction in workforce,

    (ii)   the discontinuance of a plant or operation, or

    (iii)   other similar conditions.

A qualified plan cannot provide for the payment of benefits when the unemployment results from a voluntary decision by the employee.

The Affordable Care Act and DBA

The Patient Protection and Affordable Care Act (PPACA / ACA), colloquially known as "Obamacare," and the Davis-Bacon Act (DBA) presented an interesting intersection of federal statutes. DBA regulations specifically **prohibit** the use of fringe dollars for mandatory employer taxes, for instance, contributions required by federal, state or local law. Specifically, contributions toward Social Security are not deductible as a bona fide benefit.

Section 1513 of the ACA created new Internal Revenue Code (IRC) section 4980H, which requires that Applicable Large Employers (ALEs) (50 or more full time employees) must offer their full time employees (minimum of 30 hours or work per week or 130 hours per month) and their dependents (children younger than age 26) health coverage that is affordable and provides minimum value. Alternatively, the ALE may make a payment to the Internal Revenue Service (IRS) if they don't offer this coverage and at least one full time employee purchases health insurance through an Exchange and receives the premium tax credit.

All Agency Memorandum #220 (AAM) dated March 30, 2016 clarified the intersection of DBA and ACA.

> "WHD has concluded that health benefits provided by employers

subject to the employer shared responsibility provisions are not benefits required by law within the meaning or the DBRA. Therefore, all employers, ALEs and non-ALEs, may continue to take credit for contributions to bona fide health plans as they have done in the past.[26]

Another key question that was answered in AAM 200 was whether or not employers' payment of employer shared responsibility payments to the IRS may be credited toward DBRA. They may not.

"Employers that are liable for the employer shared responsibility payment to the IRS may not credit the cost of this payment toward DBRA obligations.[29]

The fact that a health plan is a "bona fide" benefit under the DBA does not guarantee that the employer will avoid responsibility under the shared responsibility provision of the ACA. The employer must make sure that the medical plan offered is both affordable and provides minimum value under ACA regulations.

---

[26] https://www.wdol.gov/aam/aam%20220.pdf

It is the employer's decision, not the employee's, whether or not "bona fide" benefits are offered. Employers may choose to provide all employees with ACA compliant benefits even if some, or all, employees would prefer to receive other benefits or the fringes in the paycheck. [27]

Per Member Rating Requirements

Under the ACA, "composite rating" - a practice in which insurers use the rating characteristics of a group as a whole to determine an average premium rate per employee – is generally no longer permitted in the small group (fewer than 50 employees) market. Instead, insurers must use "per-member rating," under which premium rates are calculated individually for each employee.

As a result of these requirements, an employer that contributes to a health insurance plan to satisfy its obligations under the DBRA may take credit for no more than the premiums charged to the employer by the insurer for each employee at issue. For example, if an employer in the small group market chooses an insurance plan that does not offer composite premiums, but only offers

---

[27] https://www.dol.gov/whd/programs/dbra/Survey/ACAFAQs.pdf

individualized premiums on a member-by-member basis, then the amount of permissible credit will necessarily vary from employee to employee. [29]

It is important to note that employers who select insurers who charge a composite, or average, premium are able to take the composite amount of DBRA credit per employee. Even though the composite premium is derived from different per-member rates, it reflects the cost that the insurer is charging the employer to insure each employee.

Bona fide "self-funded" health benefits

A self-funded health plan is a way of structuring a health plan that enables an employer to have greater control of covered benefits and visibility of provider claims payments. An insurance company or third-party administrator typically manages provider network requirements and one of the primary benefits of self-funding is the gain in cash flow flexibility: provider claims are paid only after being incurred. (By comparison, fully insured premiums are paid to the insurance carrier each month.) However, if prevailing wage fringe dollars are to be credited toward a self-funded plan, then the dollars must be irrevocably contributed toward the plan and cannot remain an asset on the employer's balance sheet.

The key section regarding irrevocable contributions is:

> § 5.26 "* * * contribution irrevocably made * * * to a trustee or to a third person". Under the fringe benefits provisions (section 1(b)(2) of the Act) the amount of contributions for fringe benefits must be made to a trustee or to a third person irrevocably. The "third person" must be one who is not affiliated with the contractor or subcontractor. The trustee must assume the usual fiduciary

responsibilities imposed upon trustees by applicable law. The trust or fund must be set up in such a way that in no event will the contractor or subcontractor be able to recapture any of the contributions paid in or any way divert the funds to his own use or benefit.

Wage determinations generally require that wages and fringe benefit credits be calculated on a per employee basis. This is addressed in 29 CFR Part 5, Subpart B - Interpretation of the Fringe Benefits Provisions of the Davis-Bacon Act. Employees working on these types of contracts are entitled to the basic hourly rate of pay [§29 CFR 5.24] and the rate of contribution or cost for fringe benefits [§29 CFR 5.25].

Employers can fulfill their fringe benefit obligation by providing bona fide fringe benefits, making cash payments, or a combination of benefits and cash. The USDOL does not approve funded plans considered "bona fide" consistent with §29 CFR 5.25.

Therefore, to satisfy DBA fringe benefit requirements, an employer must make contributions to a third person pursuant to a bona fide plan, fund, or program and include provisions that:

- Are a legally enforceable commitment between the employer, trustee and plan administrator for the specific purpose of providing death, disability, medical and hospitalization benefits.

- Are fully-funded and entirely contractor financed and specified in writing and communicated to affected employees.
- Contain a specific formula that determines the amount of contributions and benefits.
- Are funded by irrevocable employer contributions to a trust and administered by a third party which assumes the usual fiduciary responsibilities.
- Established and operated in accordance with ERISA and is not disapproved by the IRS.
- Do not provide benefits required by other federal, state, or local laws.

Compatible with these requirements, a methodology of "self-funding" an employer's health and welfare program that operates in the following manner is compliant:

- The purpose of the single employer trust is to provide health benefits and contains provisions for the irrevocability of contributions made.
- The plan is fully-funded to the maximum employer liability of the stop-loss insurance contract.
- As specified in the Adoption Agreement, the plan is a legally enforceable obligation and a binding agreement between the adopting employer and the Plan Trustee.

- The requirements are met by the Summary of Benefits (specified in writing and communicated to employees).
- Meets the requirements of ERISA and the IRS.
- Does not provide benefits required by any other federal, state, or local law.

Site of Work

The "site of work" is where the Davis-Bacon Act (DBA) wage rates apply. Usually, this means the boundaries of the project (place or places where the construction called for in the contract will remain after work has been completed). Site of work may also refer to adjacent or "close proximity" work sites that are used exclusively or virtually exclusively for the DBA project and where a *significant* portion of the building or work will be constructed. A typical point of demarcation would be anything within one (1) mile would meet the definition of "site of work."

The "site of the work" does not include a contractor's or subcontractor's:
- Permanent home office, branch locations, fabrication plants, tool yards, etc.
- The continuing operation and location are determined without regard to a particular covered project.
- Fabrication plants, batch plants, job headquarters, tool yards, etc. that are established by a commercial materials supplier, assuming:
  - Established prior to the opening of bids for a project
  - Not located on the actual site of the work

Note: permanent, previously established facilities are not part of the "site of the work," even where the operations for a short time may be dedicated exclusively, or nearly, to the performance of a contract.

Apprenticeship and Training

DOL Bureau of Apprenticeship and Training (BAT). Apprentices and trainees are paid according to the approved program pay schedules. Enrolled apprentices are the only workers who may be paid less than the prevailing wage rate shown in the wage determination. For example, pre-apprentices must be paid the prevailing wage since they are not enrolled in the BAT apprenticeship program.

Apprentices are laborers not listed on wage determinations (WD) and are permitted to work on covered projects and be paid less than the journey level WD rate only when:

- Individually registered in an approved apprenticeship or training program;
- Paid the hourly rate required by the apprenticeship or training program;
- Paid the FB's specified in the approved program; if the program is silent, the full amount of FB's listed on the WD should be utilized; and
- Within the allowable ratio specified in approved program for the number of apprentices or trainees to journeymen.

Best Practices: Demonstrating Compliance

- Use the proper classifications for the work performed.
- Pay the wages and benefits required by the contract WD.
- Demonstrating compliance starts with recordkeeping! It is easier to be successful in compliance when all recordkeeping requirements are followed and records are accurate.
- Ensure required notifications are posted.

Recordkeeping Requirements

Contractors must maintain payroll and basic records for all laborers and mechanics during the course of the work and for a period of three years thereafter. Keeping accurate, contemporaneous records will sufficiently rebut allegations of non-compliance.

Records to be maintained include:
- Name, address, and Social Security number of each employee.
- Each employee's work classifications.
- Hourly rates of pay, including rates of contributions or costs anticipated for fringe benefits or their cash equivalents.
- Daily and weekly numbers of hours worked and workers sign their time records to affirm agreement.
- Deductions made.

- Actual wages paid.
- Make corrections when errors are discovered and report them immediately.
- If applicable,
  - Detailed information regarding various fringe benefit plans and programs, including records that show that the plan or program has been communicated in writing to the laborers and mechanics affected.
  - Detailed information concerning approved trainee apprenticeship programs.
  - Review payroll records submitted by subcontractors.

Another best practice is ensuring that your bid includes language about prevailing wage. For instance, if you are bidding under prevailing wage, it is helpful to include the job classifications, wage, and fringe benefit rates you used to develop your quote. Conversely, if you believe that prevailing wage does not apply, you should state that in your contract.

When in doubt ask the contracting officer for help and clarification.

DOL Investigations

In advance of a DOL inquiry, contractors would be advised to:

1. Examine closely all written job descriptions to ensure that the worker classification accurately reflects the work to be done.
2. Ensure that required payroll records and recordkeeping retention policies and procedures are current, accurate, and compliant.
3. Utilize a timekeeping system that allows for the convenient entry of all hours worked.
4. Develop a formal program for reporting and resolving employee wage concerns.
5. Conduct wage & hour audits — ideally by in-house or outside legal counsel to protect the findings under the attorney-client privilege.
6. Familiarize Managers with Key Concepts of Wage & Hour Laws and your procedures for DOL Inspections.
7. Apply policies consistently.

What will a DOL auditor do?

A visit from a DOL investigator may be prompted by a complaint filed with their offices or may be the result of a targeted effort by the DOL pursuant to your DBA work. The DOL visits construction project sites and investigates the construction companies it finds working on the project. "As long as someone at the site grants permission to the interviewers (that someone is likely to be a project superintendent or manager who represents the owner or general contractor), your employees might be interviewed by the DOL with no knowledge or preparation on your part."[28]

DOL auditors:
- May or may not give advance notice of a site visit
- Will likely want to talk to employees. However, employees are not obligated to talk to auditor
- Will likely want to see payroll and other applicable records
- Will likely want to observe the site of work

Employers should:
- Ask what the focus of the investigation is.
- Be respectful and accommodating.

---

[28] https://corporate.findlaw.com/human-resources/is-your-company-prepared-for-a-visit-from-the-department-of.html

- Ask the auditor to provide a summary of the results of the investigation.

Penalties for Non-compliance

Per the Department of Labor:

> *Contractors or subcontractors found to have disregarded their obligations to employees under the Davis-Bacon Act, or found to be "in aggravated or willful violation" of any of the related Acts, may be subject to debarment from future contracts for up to three years. In addition, contract payments may be withheld in sufficient amounts to satisfy liabilities for unpaid wages and for liquidated damages that result from overtime violations of the Contract Work Hours and Safety Standards Act (CWHSSA). Breach of the required contract clauses under the Davis-Bacon and related Acts and CWHSSA may also be grounds for termination of the contract.*

> *Contractors and subcontractors may challenge the Wage and Hour Division's determinations of violations and debarment before*

an Administrative Law Judge. Contractors and subcontractors may appeal decisions by Administrative Law Judges to the Department's Administrative Review Board (ARB). ARB determinations on violations may be appealed to and are enforceable through the federal courts.

Falsification of the required certified payroll records or any kickback of wages may subject a contractor or subcontractor to civil or criminal prosecution, the penalty for which may be fines and/or imprisonment.[29]

---

[29] https://webapps.dol.gov/elaws/elg/dbra.htm#Penalites

Executive Order 13658, Establishing a Minimum Wage for Contractors

On September 26, 2018, the Department of Labor published a Final Rule in the Federal Register: Minimum Wage for Contractors; Updating Regulations to Reflect Executive Order 13838.

Beginning January 1, 2019, President Obama's Executive Order 13658 minimum wage rate is $10.60 per hour (83 FR 44906). This Executive Order minimum wage rate generally must be paid to workers performing work on or in connection with covered contracts. Additionally, tipped employees performing work on or in connection with covered contracts generally must be paid a minimum cash wage of $7.40 per hour.

Employee Communications (Posters)

Employers must post several posters at the job site; it is _not_ compliant to have a binder with the following notices.

Employee Rights Under the Davis-Bacon Act

Every employer performing work covered by the labor standards of the Davis-Bacon Act must post a notice that includes applicable wage determinations at the site of the work in a prominent and accessible place where it may be easily seen by employees.

"Equal Employment Opportunity is the Law" (EEO)

Executive Order 11246 prohibits certain federal contractors and subcontractors from discriminating in employment decisions on the basis of race, color, religion, sex, sexual orientation, gender identity or national origin.

Executive Order 11246 protects applicants and employees from employer disciplinary actions, including termination of employment, for employees asking about, discussing or disclosing their own pay or the pay of their co-workers.

Pay Transparency Nondiscrimination Provision

Executive Order 11246 also requires employers to post the Pay Transparency Nondiscrimination Provision poster and include it in employee manuals and handbooks. The poster and information provides applicants and employees notice that the employer will not discriminate against them for inquiring about, discussing, or disclosing their pay or, in certain circumstances, the pay of their co-workers.

Executive Order 13496: Notification of Employee Rights under Federal Labor Laws

Federal contractors and subcontractors are required to inform employees of their rights under the National Labor Relations Act (NLRA), the primary law governing relations between unions and employers in the private sector. See 29 CFR Part 471. The notice, prescribed in the Department of Labor's regulations, informs employees of federal contractors and subcontractors of their rights under the NLRA to organize and bargain collectively with their employers and to engage in other protected concerted activity.

OSHA Job Safety and Health: It's the Law

Informs workers of their rights under the Occupational Safety and Health Act. All covered employers are required to display the poster in their workplace.

Your Rights Under USERRA

Employers are required to provide to employees entitled to the rights and benefits under the Uniformed Services Employment and Reemployment Rights Act (USERRA), a notice of the rights, benefits, and obligations of such persons and such employers under USERRA. Employers may provide the notice, by posting it where employee notices are customarily placed. However, employers are free to provide the notice to employees in other ways that will minimize costs while ensuring that the full text of the notice is provided (e.g. by handing / mailing out the notice, or distributing the notice electronically).

Contract Work Hours and Safety Standards Act

The Contract Work Hours and Safety Standards Act (CWHSSA), pronounced "qua-sa," is a Davis-Bacon Related Act (DBRA) that requires time plus one-half for overtime (O/T) hours that exceed forty (40) hours in a work week. The contractor can determine the work week by selecting any consistent seven (7) day period. For instance, work weeks may begin on a Sunday or Monday.

CWHSSA determines that wages must be paid for both standard time (S/T) and overtime (O/T) hours. However, fringe benefit payments are not included in the overtime (O/T) rate of pay.[30]

As an example, if the fringe is $10 and the base is $40 the contractor would have to pay $10 for all hours worked and $60 ($40 x 1.5) on each hour of O/T.

---

[30] Field Operations Manual 15f11(d)

The Copeland Act (Anti-Kickback Act)

This related act makes it a crime for anyone to require any laborer employed on a federal, or federally assisted, project to kickback any part of their wages and requires the _**weekly submittal**_ of _**Certified Payroll Reports (CPRs)**_.

The Fair Labor Standards Act (FLSA)

The FLSA contains federal minimum wage rates and overtime (O/T) requirements that apply to any labor performed and may pre-empt the Davis-Bacon wage rates.

> *The FLSA sets minimum wage, overtime pay, recordkeeping, and youth employment standards for employment subject to its provisions. Unless exempt, covered employees must be paid at least the minimum wage and not less than one and one-half times their regular rates of pay for overtime hours worked.*[31]

In the case of the government contracts statutes, contract funds may be withheld for violations under Davis-Bacon and Related Acts, and Contract Work Hours and Safety Standards Act. Administrative hearings, or in some cases court action, may be initiated to recover back pay under these laws. In addition, liquidated damages may be assessed for certain violations. Violators of these laws may also lose their federal contracts and be declared ineligible for future contracts for a specified period.

---

[31] https://www.dol.gov/whd/regs/compliance/whdfs21.pdf

State Prevailing Wage & Little Davis-Bacon Laws

Washington DC and twenty-seven states currently have statewide prevailing wage laws, while twenty-three states do not have prevailing wage laws.

The following states have state prevailing wage requirements: Alaska, California, Connecticut, Delaware, Hawaii, Illinois, Maine, Maryland, Massachusetts, Michigan, Minnesota, Missouri, Montana, Nebraska, Nevada, New Jersey, New Mexico, New York, Ohio, Oregon, Pennsylvania, Rhode Island, Tennessee, Texas, Vermont, Washington, Washington, D.C., and Wyoming.[32]

States without prevailing wage tend to be in the South and Mid-West and include: Alabama, Arizona, Arkansas, Colorado, Florida, Georgia, Idaho, Indiana, Iowa, Kansas, Kentucky, Louisiana, Mississippi, New Hampshire, North Carolina, North Dakota, Oklahoma, South Carolina, South Dakota, Utah, Virginia, West Virginia, and Wisconsin.

---

[32] https://www.dol.gov/whd/state/dollar.htm

California Prevailing Wage

California prevailing wage laws and regulations reflect an intention by state leaders to be at the forefront of prevailing wage regulation and enforcement. Simply put, California has many more complexities and regulations than most other states.

In California, the prevailing wage project cost threshold (including local or municipal projects) is one thousand dollars ($1,000). Remarkably, a project bid need not specify prevailing wage to have prevailing wage requirements apply. Government entities will sometimes provide a purchase order for an amount over $1,000, but it is up to the contractor to recognize that prevailing wage applies.

California prevailing wage rates are updated and communicated twice per calendar year on February 22nd and August 22nd by the **Department of Industrial Relations (DIR)**, with the revised rate effective ten (10) days later. As with all prevailing wage rates, California prevailing wage rates reflect the *minimum* that must be paid.

The first advertised bid date, often referred to as the "call for bids," is the correct wage determination rate to be used. A project that is first advertised on August 10th, with a bid opening date of September 1st and work that begins October 1st, would require the contractor to use the rates in force as of March since the initial bid notice was prior to the September 1st effective date of the revised wage rates.

Deborah E.G. Wilder, in her book *What Every Contractor Should Know about Prevailing Wages*, states:

> *Note: there are many contractors and even some local agencies that are confused over the proper determination to be used. Some think it is the wage determination at the time of the bid or the time that the contractor actually starts work on the project. Others think that when each new prevailing wage determination is published by the state, the wage rate needs to be changed. However, the California Labor Code and accompanying regulations provide that it is the first day of the advertisement for call with bids which controls.*
>
> *The decision to use the wage rate available at the time bids are first*

advertised makes a lot of sense. A contractor needs to know the labor cost for a project. In order to do that, the contractor has to know which prevailing wage rates are going to apply so that an accurate price can be quoted. It would make no sense to hold a contractor to wage rates issued on the date of the bid or even after the bid was opened.[33]

Site of Work in California

Another unique aspect of California prevailing wage law, which is different from federal DBA, is the definition of a temporary work facility. While federal regulations prescribe "adjacent or nearly adjacent" [see Chapter: Site of Work], California has no distinction but instead relies on whether or not the facility is temporary and dedicated to the production of work for the prevailing wage covered job. (A site that is permanent and does not use exclusively for prevailing wage covered labor is exempt from the regulations.)

Reading a CA Wage Determination

The Total Hourly Rate comprises the Basic Hourly Rate, Health & Welfare, Pension, Vacation/Holiday, Training and/or Other.

---

[33] AuthorHouse 2010

When interpreting the California wage determination a key section is the Basic Hourly Rate (BHR), which is the amount that must be paid to the employee in their paycheck. A contractor must pay each worker no less than the stated BHR in his or her paycheck - "dipping" into the base is not permitted as it is under a DBA federal contract.

While the California wage determination lists separate amounts for the Health & Welfare and Pension, these amounts may be combined and discharged into a single bona fide benefit. For instance, in the below example the amount of H&W, Pension, V/H and "Other Payments" should be looked at as one fringe allocation to be used towards benefits and/or additional wages. In the below example, $27.81 may be contributed entirely into a bona fide retirement plan.[34] If the employer does not have fringe benefits that meet or exceed the total of the amount listed in the wage determination, then the difference must be added to the employee's paycheck.

I T: LOS ANGELES COUNTY INATION: LOS-2019-1						EMPLOYER PAYMENTS				STRAIGHT-TIME	
CRAFT (JOURNEY LEVEL)	ISSUE DATE	EXPIRATION DATE	BASIC HOURLY RATE	HEALTH AND WELFARE	PENSION	VACATION/ HOLIDAY	TRAINING	OTHER PAYMENTS	HOURS	TOTAL HOURLY RATE
INSIDE VIREMAN, RADIO MONITOR TECHNICIAN	2/22/2019	06/30/2019*	45.200	12.740 Ø	14.570 R	-	0.710	0.500	8.0	75.080

---

[34] California Public Works Manual, August 2016

Some contractors look at the attached WD and think they are limited to $14.57 for a retirement plan, for example. Not true. If a contractor is calculating credit for health insurance on their own and come up with a $3 per hour in annualized cost, that is all the credit they can take, not $12.74.

Any amount under "Training" ($0.71/hour in this case) must go to an accredited apprenticeship program, or to the California Apprenticeship Council (CAC). It may not be paid on the check or to another program except for a couple of very small exceptions.

Reporting Fringe Benefit Payments

The Statement of Employer Payments (CA form: PW 26) is essentially a fringe benefit statement and records key information about the employer's bona fide benefits plan, including the name of the plan, classifications used, and the frequency of contributions. Like the CPR, PW 26 is submitted under penalty of perjury.

Prevailing wage in California also frequently applies to private work.

CA Labor Code 17xx spells out the particulars, but some examples include:

1. 50%+ of project square footage is leased by a public entity prior to construction contract

2. Construction is done per state criteria (even if the government's lease is entered into post contract)
3. Construction of/on an acute care hospital if the work is paid for from a conduit revenue bond (with some exceptions)
4. Construction of renewable energy where 50% or more of the capacity will be purchased by a government entity
5. Affordable housing projects
6. Private contracts may simply require PW
7. Individual purchase orders under $1,000 are typically grouped together when subject to an ongoing service contract.

Contractor Registration with DIR

California requires contractors to register with the Department of Industrial Relations (D.I.R.) in order to bid on prevailing wage construction, unless the project is under $25,000 or $15,000 for maintenance. The fee is currently $400 and must be renewed each year on July 1st irrespective of the date of your company's initial registration.

Hawaii Prevailing Wage

In the state of Hawaii, the Hawaii Prepaid Health law, enacted in 1974, requires all employers to pay a portion of the medical insurance premiums for their employees who work more than 20 hours per week.

Per the DOL West Regional Office,

> *"It has been our policy to permit contractors and subcontractors to take full credit towards their Davis-Bacon prevailing wage obligations in the State of Hawaii for contributions made to bona fide health insurance plans."*[35]

Although the federal DBA permits quarterly deposits to a bona fide plan, the state of HI requires deposits to be made no less often than monthly for any benefit. Obviously, if a contractor is working on a military base in HI, they can follow the DBA rule, but we encourage Hawaiian contractors to contribute at least monthly to avoid any confusion down the road.

---

[35] Mr. Alfred B Robinson, Jr. Senior Policy Advisor, U.S. Department of Labor, Employment Standards Division, Washington, D.C. 20210

Illinois Prevailing Wage

The contactor/subcontractor who wishes to take credit for health and welfare, pension/retirement, training, or vacation benefits must maintain records to verify any plans for which the contractor/subcontractor participates. The records required for substantiation include, but are not limited to, records that document contributions made, total contribution requirements, policies including eligibility requirements, vesting provisions, and calculation of fringe benefit credit taken, if any.

Examples are as follows:

First example: If a contractor contributes $520 per month for single insurance coverage and the employee works on a full-time basis, then the effective annual contribution rate is determined by dividing $6240 ($520 x 12) by 2080 (the number of hours a full-time employee would typically work in a year) which equals $3.00 per hour. If the health and welfare portion of the prevailing wage is $5.05 per hour, the contractor/subcontractor can take a credit of $3.00 per hour and must pay $2.05 ($5.05-$3.00) additional on the hourly base wage.

Second example: If a contractor contributed to a bona fide fund $5.05 for every hour worked, the effective annual rate of contribution is $5.05. If the health and welfare portion of the prevailing wage is $5.05 per hour, the contractor/subcontractor can take a credit of $5.05 per hour and does not have to pay any additional amount on the hourly base wage.

Third example: If a contractor contributed to a bona fide health and welfare fund $6.05 for every hour an employee works, the effective annual rate of contribution is $6.05. If the allowable health and welfare portion of the prevailing wage is $5.05 per hour, the contractor/subcontractor can take a credit of $5.05 per hour. The contractor/subcontractor cannot receive an additional credit of $1.00 ($5.05 - $6.05), which can apply to reducing the hourly base wage that must be paid.

The same formula applies to 401k and pension plans, annuities, training, and vacation where applicable.

Delaware Prevailing Wage

In Delaware cash paid directly to an employee in lieu of fringe benefits as part of Davis-Bacon or prevailing wage jobs is excluded for workers' compensation premium calculation purposes. However, the job specified minimum wage paid to the employee is included. An employer will usually have certified prevailing wage payroll sheets for each prevailing wage job that differentiate between the wage and the fringe benefit, but only the fringe benefit portion may be deducted.

Massachusetts Prevailing Wage

Massachusetts G. L ch. 149, §§ 26-27H, permits employers to deduct contributions to bona fide health and welfare plans from the hourly prevailing wage rate. Under no circumstances may an employer deduct more from employee's prevailing wage than is actually contributed to a bona fide plan on his or her behalf.

It is customary for employers to use a pre-specified hourly deduction for contributions to bona fide health and welfare plans based on two factors: the monthly cost of the health and welfare plan and the customary work hours per month (assuming payments to plans are made monthly). By dividing the customary work hours per month into the cost of the plan, employers arrive at their pre-specified hourly deduction to be subtracted from the employee's prevailing rate.

An employer may use 160 hour (four weeks times 40 hours) as the customary work hours per month. Other methods, such as your suggestion to use the annual hours worked, are not necessarily incorrect, and may be used as long as the hourly deduction for each employee accurately reflects the employer's contribution to his or her bona fide benefit plan. Employers must ensure that the sum total of all pre-specified hourly deductions in a payment period does not exceed the payment or premium paid to a bona fide plan on the employee's behalf.

In more simple terms: Employers may use any method they wish for calculating hourly contributions to health and welfare plans as long as those contributions do not exceed the cost of the plan.[36]

---

[36] Opinion Letter PW-2002-04-10.02.02, Ronald E. Maranian, Program Manager

New York Prevailing Wage

An early chapter in this book titled, "Annualization" explains in great depth the concept of annualizing benefit plan contributions. In essence, monthly premiums are multiplied by 12 (months) and divided by 2,080 (40 hours per week times 52 weeks) to calculate a consistent hourly amount. Employers may take credit toward required fringe benefits according to the prevailing wage schedule as long as the same per hour amount is paid by the employer even when not working on a prevailing wage job. In other words, total annual contributions per employee are divided by the total annual hours worked by that employee, on both public and private jobs.

The state of New York will generally look to the time frame used by the employer, i.e. fiscal year, calendar year, plan year, etc. If the employer has not utilized a specific time frame to calculate their credit, in most instances the state will use a calendar year. An employer needs to be consistent in using the same twelve-month period year to year.

1. The hourly amount can be provided in cash in the employee's weekly paycheck when working on a public work project. Paying the required supplement amount weekly in cash with the employee's wages fulfills the requirement under Article 8; or

2. A contribution can be made to a bona fide benefit plan on behalf of the employee. If this option is chosen and the contributions are not made on an hourly basis for all hours worked, both public and private, then the hourly cash credit the employer receives for supplement contributions must be determined (i.e. annualization). Once that credit is determined, if there is any deficiency between the required supplement amount and the hourly credit amount, it must be made up weekly along with employee's wages.
3. If, pursuant to a collective bargaining agreement, contributions are made for all hours worked (public and private) and are at least the amount shown in the wage schedule, the requirements of the law have been met.

Example A
Total annual employer contribution to benefit plan(s) on behalf of individual employee = $5000

The individual employee works 1000 hours on a public work project and 1000 hours on a private project for a total of 2000 hours.

$5,000 contribution divided by / 2000 total hours worked = 2.50 per hour credit

The employer is responsible to pay the difference between the credit for contributed amounts, $2.50 in this case, and amounts called for in the prevailing wage schedule.

For example;
If the employee worked as a carpenter for 20 hours and the carpenter supplement amount in the prevailing wage schedule is $10, subtract the $2.50 credit from $10. The carpenter would be owed $7.50 in cash for every hour worked as a carpenter on the public work project.

If the same employee also worked 15 hours as a laborer and the laborer supplement amount is $7.50, subtract the $2.50 credit from the $7.50. The laborer would be owed $5.00 in cash for each hour worked as a laborer on the public work project.

Example B
Employer pays $150 per month in health insurance premiums, $50 per month for dental premiums:

$150 x 12 months = $1800 paid per year for health insurance
$50 x 12 months = $600 paid per year for dental insurance

Total annual contribution = $2400

The employee worked 2080 hours (52 weeks x 40 hours) during the year on both public and private work (52 - 40 hour weeks)

Divide the employer contribution to the plan ($2400) by the total number of hours worked during the year (2080 hours) to calculate the per-hour credit against supplement, $1.15 in this case.

If the employee worked as an operating engineer and the operating engineer supplement in the prevailing wage schedule is $11.50 per hour, subtract the $1.15 credit from $11.50. The operating engineer would be owed $10.35 in cash for the hours worked as an operating engineer on the public work project.

Does an employer receive credit for contributions to plans that have waiting periods to qualify for health insurance benefits or pension plans with extended vesting schedules?

Yes. The New York State Department of Labor (NYS DOL) does not regulate waiting periods, vesting schedules, etc. That responsibility lies with the United States Department of Labor's Employee Benefit Security Administration.

The NYS DOL will verify that:
1. The plan is a bona fide plan; and
2. The employee is a plan participant; and

3. The monies claimed to have been contributed on behalf of each employee have in fact been contributed.

Would a cafeteria plan comply with the annualization requirement?

Yes. A true cafeteria plan, where the total dollar value of the supplement amount is provided to the employee and the employee is provided the option or vehicle to purchase their own benefits, is considered the same as cash.[37]

General Contractor Liability

NYS Labor Law § 223 Holds General Contractors vicariously liable for underpayments by subcontractors. Additionally, the G.C. may also be liable for a 25% civil penalty levied against subcontractors.

---

[37] NYSDOL - Bureau of Public Work

Works Cited

What Every Contractor Should Know About Prevailing Wages, Deborah E.G. Wilder

Bernstein, David, *The Davis-Bacon Act: Let's Bring Jim Crow to an End* (PDF), Cato Institute

Schulman, Stuart, "The Case Against the Davis-Bacon Act", *Government-Union Review* (Winter 1983)

Bernstein, David E. (2001), "Prevailing-Wage Laws", *Only One Place of Redress: African Americans, Labor Regulations and the Court from Reconstruction to the New Deal*, Duke University Press, ISBN 978-0822325833

Glassman, Sarah; Head, Michael; Tuerck, David G.; Bachman, Paul (2008), The Federal Davis-Bacon Act: The Prevailing Mismeasure of Wages (PDF), Beacon Hill Institute

James H. Watz, Labor Law, 6 B.C.L. Rev. 242 (1965), http://lawdigitalcommons.bc.edu/bclr/vol6/iss2/8

29 CFR 1.3

Presentation of Davis Bacon Wage Survey Process – https://www.dol.gov/whd/programs/dbra/wd-10.htm

https://www.dol.gov/whd/state/dollar.htm

https://www.smithcurrie.com/publications/com
mon-sense-contract-law/project-labor-
agreements-in-public-and-private-contracting/

https://www.nationalbcc.org/news/latest-
news/2895-coalition-letter-to-peotus-trump-on-
project-labor-agreement-policy

Senate Report No. 1518, 1960–2 C.B. 753 at 754.

https://www.ecfr.gov/cgi-bin/text-
idx?SID=7ae1f410a0cc51b5054e09676ad67ae6&
mc=true&node=se13.1.124_1103&rgn=div8

https://www.fedgovcontracts.com/chap11.pdf
□ https://www.everycrsreport.com/reports/94-
908.html#_Toc228614935

https://digitalcommons.ilr.cornell.edu/cgi/view
content.cgi?referer=https://www.google.com/&
httpsredir=1&article=1232&context=key_workpl
ace

https://www.nytimes.com/1986/05/15/opinion/
reduce-the-pork-in-davis-bacon.html

https://timesmachine.nytimes.com/timesmachi
ne/1913/02/21/100255394.pdf

https://www.dol.gov/whd/forms/wh347.pdf

Made in United States
North Haven, CT
21 September 2022

24405340R00055